KINGFISHER READERS

level **2**

Where We Live

Brenda Stones and
Thea Feldman

KINGFISHER
NEW YORK

KINGFISHER
LONDON & NEW YORK

Distributed in the U.S. and Canada by Macmillan,
175 Fifth Ave., New York, NY 10010

Library of Congress Cataloging-in-Publication data has been applied for.

Series editor: Thea Feldman
Literacy consultant: Ellie Costa, Bank St. College, New York

ISBN: 978-0-7534-6901-9 (HB)
ISBN: 978-0-7534-6902-6 (PB)

Kingfisher books are available for special promotions and
premiums. For details contact: Special Markets Department,
Macmillan, 175 Fifth Ave., New York, NY 10010.

For more information, please visit
www.kingfisherbooks.com

Printed in China
9 8 7 6 5 4
4TR/0216/UG/WKT/105MA

Picture credits
The Publisher would like to thank the following for permission to reproduce their material. Every care has
been taken to trace copyright holders. However, if there have been unintentional omissions or failure to trace
copyright holders, we apologize and will, if informed, endeavor to make corrections in any future edition.
Top = t; Bottom = b; Center = c; Left = l; Right = r.
Cover Shutterstock/June Marie Sobrito; Pages 4 Photolibrary/Uppercut Images; 5t Photolibrary/Asia
Image Group; 5b Photolibrary/GoGo; 6 Shutterstock/Elena Elisseeva; 7t Shutterstock/Felix Mizionikov;
7b Shutterstock/LianeM; 8 Shutterstock/SF photo; 9t Shutterstock/Darko Zeljkovic; 9b Photolibrary/Flirt
Collection; 10–11 Getty/Panoramic Images; 11t Corbis/Adam Woolfitt; 11b Photolibrary/Lineair; 12 Getty/
Image Bank; 13 Corbis/Danny Lehman; 14 Shutterstock; 15t Photolibrary/Age Fotostock; 15b Alamy/
Thomas Cockrem; 16 Shutterstock/prism88; 17t & 17b Nutshell Media /Sue Cunningham; 18t Shutterstock/
Kruchankova Maya; 18b Shutterstock/John Leung; 19 Shutterstock/Vladimir Melnik; 20 Corbis/John Miller/
Robert Harding World Imagery; 21 Shutterstock/Sergii Korshun; 22–23 Shutterstock/kirych; 23t Photolibrary/
Ingram Publishing; 23b Corbis/Lindsay Hebberd; 24–25 Corbis/VStock LLC/Tetra Images; 24t Shutterstock/
Dmitrijs Bindemanis; 26–27 Photolibrary/Bios; 27 Shutterstock/Robert Hackett; 28–29 Photolibrary/Jon
Arnold Travel; 29t Corbis/Pascal Deloche/Godong; 30t Shutterstock/Jose Wilson Araujo; 30b Corbis/Michael
S. Yamashita; 31t Corbis/Gavin Heller; 31c Photolibrary/Photononstop; 31b Shutterstock/Lance Bellers.

Contents

At home

Your **home** is where you live.

You eat, sleep, read, play, stay safe, and much more in your home.

There are many kinds of homes.

Let's visit some!

Kinds of homes

Many people live in **houses**.

A house has at least one home in it.

Some houses are all in a row.

Some houses stand by themselves.

Many people live in **apartments**.

Apartment buildings have many homes inside.

Apartment buildings can be tall!

In a town

In a town or city
many houses and apartment buildings
are built near each other.

Places to work, schools,
and stores are nearby too.

If you live in a town,
your friends might live near you!

In the country

Some people live in the country.

There are fewer homes there than in the city.

This farm is in the country.

A **village** is a small group of homes, stores, schools, and other buildings in the country.

By the water

Many people live near lakes and rivers.

They use the water in many ways.

In some places,
people do their wash
in the water.

In Venice, Italy, people use boats to get around their city!

Many people live near the sea.

Some of them own boats.

They may use their boats
to catch fish.

Some homes are built over the water.

A **houseboat** is a home *in* the water!

Wood and more

Many homes are built
out of wood.

Do you like this wooden house?

Some roofs are made
out of **thatch**.

Thatch is dried plant parts.

Most windows
are made of glass.

Brick homes

Many homes are built with bricks.

Most bricks are made of baked clay.

Some bricks are made of baked mud.

This **palace** in **Yemen** has mud bricks.

Keeping cool

If you live in a hot place,
your home can keep you cool.

You can close the **shutters**
to keep out the sun.

Fountains and pools of water
make the air feel cooler.

Buildings painted light colors
do not take in the sun's heat
as much as buildings
painted dark colors.

Staying warm

In very cold places
homes have thick walls and roofs.

The cold air stays outside,
and the warm air stays inside.

Some houses have fireplaces
to make it extra warm and cozy!

Rainy places

In places where it rains a lot,
you will see many slanted roofs.

The rain runs right off the roof.

But, if it rains too much,
rivers can overflow.

Homes near rivers may be flooded.

Dry places

Some people live in places
that have very little water.

They get water from a well.

Elsewhere,
some people
collect rainwater
in tanks to use
for things like
watering a garden.

Homes on the move

Some people live in a tent
in the desert.

When they move, they take the tent.

Other people drive mobile homes.

Their homes travel with them
    from place to place.

Welcome home!

At the end of every day
it is good to come home.

What kind of home
do you live in?

Glossary

apartments homes in a building with more than one home

home a place where people live

houses buildings that each have at least one home inside

houseboat a boat that is a home

palace a large home built for a king or other ruler

shutters covers for windows that keep out the sun

thatch dried plant parts

village a small group of homes and other buildings in the country

Yemen a country in the Middle East